Steph.____ _____

Christopher Hampton was born in the Azores in 1946.
He wrote his first play, *When Did You Last See My
Mother?*, at the age of eighteen. Since then, his plays
have included *The Philanthropist, Savages, Tales from
Hollywood, Les Liaisons Dangereuses, White Chameleon,
The Talking Cure* and *Appomattox*. He previously
collaborated with Don Black and Andrew Lloyd Webber
on the musical of *Sunset Boulevard*, and has translated
plays by Ibsen, Molière, von Horváth, Chekhov and
Yasmina Reza (including *Art, Life × 3*, and *God of
Carnage*). His television work includes adaptations of
The History Man and *Hotel du Lac*. His screenplays
include *The Honorary Consul, The Good Father,
Dangerous Liaisons, Mary Reilly, Total Eclipse, The
Quiet American, Atonement, Cheri, A Dangerous
Method, Carrington, The Secret Agent* and *Imagining
Argentina*, the last three of which he also directed.

Don Black, a former stand-up comedian, made his West
End debut as a lyricist on the musical *Billy*. He has
previously worked with Andrew Lloyd Webber on the
shows *Song and Dance, Aspects of Love* and *Sunset
Boulevard*. His awards include an Oscar and five Academy
Award nominations. He has written five James Bond title
songs and was recently inducted into the Songwriters
Hall of Fame.

STEPHEN WARD

THE MUSICAL

Christopher Hampton and Don Black

MUSIC BY
Andrew Lloyd Webber

[signature]

ff

FABER & FABER

First published in 2013
by Faber and Faber Limited
74–77 Great Russell Street, London WC1B 3DA

Typeset by Country Setting, Kingsdown, Kent CT14 8ES
Printed and bound by CPI Group (UK) Ltd, Croydon, CR0 4YY

A CIP record for this book
is available from the British Library

ISBN 978–0–571–31451–5

2 4 6 8 10 9 7 5 3 1

Stephen Ward was first presented at the Aldwych Theatre, London, on 3 December 2013. The cast was as follows:

Stephen Ward Alexander Hanson
Christine Keeler Charlotte Spencer
Mandy Rice-Davies Charlotte Blackledge

Astor / Griffith-Jones Anthony Calf
Rachman / Journalist 3 Martin Callaghan
Lucky Gordon Ricardo Coke-Thomas
Ivanov / Journalist 1 / Herbert Ian Conningham
Murray's Girl / Ronna Kate Coyston
President Ayub Khan Jason Denton
Profumo / Reggie Kray / Judge Daniel Flynn
Man in Mask / Brooke / Clore / Burge / Rawlinson
    Julian Forsyth
Murray's Girl / Bronwen / Vickie Amy Griffiths
Murray / Journalist 2 / Diggs Christopher Howell
Redmayne / Hollis / Ronnie Kray Paul Kemble
Murray's Girl / Mariella Emma Kate Nelson
Valerie / Mrs Huish Joanna Riding
Johnny Edgecombe Wayne Robinson
Ensemble Carl Sanderson
Murray's Girl Emily Squibb
Hod / Boothby / Hobson / Simpson John Stacey
Murray's Girl / Dance Captain Helen Ternent
Murray's Crooner Tim Walton

Other parts played by members of the company

Musicians

Rob Eckland (*keyboard 1*), Mark Aspinall (*keyboard 2*),
Alex Parker (*keyboard 3*), Ryan Habberfield (*guitars*),
Johnny Copland (*bass guitar/double bass*), Dave Elliott
(*drums/percussion*), Amy May (*violin/viola*), Sarah
Manship (*flutes*)

Music Andrew Lloyd Webber
Book and Lyrics Christopher Hampton, Don Black
Director Richard Eyre
Choreographer Stephen Mear
Set and Costume Designer Rob Howell
Lighting Designer Peter Mumford
Sound Designer Paul Groothuis
Projection Design John Driscoll
Music Supervisor and Music Director Graham Hurman
Associate Music Director Alex Parker
Hair and Make-Up Campbell Young
Associate Director Adrian Sarple
Associate Choreographer Steven Harris

Characters

Bronwen, Viscountess Astor

President Ayub Khan

Valerie Hobson

Three Journalists

Brigadier Martin Redmayne
Chief Whip

Sir Peter Rawlinson
Solicitor-General

Sir John Hobson
Attorney-General

Henry Brooke
Home Secretary

Sir Roger Hollis
Head of MI5

Sir Joseph Simpson
Commissioner of Police

Chiref Inspector Samuel Herbert

Detective Sergeant John Diggs

Vickie Barrett

Ronna Ricardo

James Burge

Mervyn Griffith-Jones

Sir Archibald Marshall
Judge

STEPHEN WARD

Locations

ACT ONE

ACT TWO

Act One

*The Chamber of Horrors in the Blackpool branch of
Louis Tussaud's: murky light, no public, just the wax
statues. It's sometime in the late sixties. The usual
unappetising suspects are lined up: Jack the Ripper,
Vlad the Impaler and the standard motley gang of Nazis.
Among them is a slightly incongruous figure: a dapper
middle-aged man in dinner jacket and black tie.
Suddenly, shockingly, he moves: indeed, he takes a silver
cigarette case out of his pocket, extracts a cigarette, taps
it on the case, lights it, inhales gratefully and steps out of
line, greeting the audience with a friendly smile. This is
Stephen Ward. His voice is exceptionally warm and
seductive.*

Ward I don't mind admitting the last place I expected to
finish up was as an exhibit in the Chamber of Horrors.
And not even at the main HQ, but in Blackpool, if you
please: nowhere to be found on my long list of desirable
places to spend the weekend. And yet, not so very long ago,
I had a fair claim to be the most popular man in London.

*He moves towards us, shaking his head ruminatively;
then looks up again, smiling, full of charm, the soul of
bonhomie.*

Stephen Ward, your friendly osteopath
I can fix your lower back for you
Also known for high-class portraiture
And you'll find out that's not all I do

Winston Churchill, Ava Gardner,
Different contours, same predicament

3

Gandhi was another regular
Called me his 'preferred medicament'

I invented a new way of life
Some might call it unconventional
All that stuffy post-war Englishness
I liked something more consensual

You'll be wondering what I'm doing here
Stuck between Hitler and the acid-bath murderer
Let me warn you it's the consequence
If you get up the nose of the establishment

If you give them what they're looking for
They'll be grateful, they'll be awfully nice
But if you should step across the line
You'll become a human sacrifice

Friends could never understand the girls who caught
    my eye
Shopgirls, models, working girls, I'd have them all
    come by
Strange behaviour you may think, but tolerance is blind
All I ever cared about was simply being kind

I tried marriage, didn't go for it
I liked freedom and diversity
Mixed with all sorts, tarts and royalty
And of course the young and beautiful

Portraits of the Duke of Edinburgh
Jolly threesomes in Belgravia
Weekends in some stately country house
With assorted misbehaviour

All this was my life
Limitless delights
All the girls
And all the parties
All the amazing nights

Self-indulgence is permissible
But one day you'll have to pay the price
I suppose I stepped across the line
And became a human sacrifice

They will bring you down unless your heart's as
  cold as ice
Nothing they like better than a human sacrifice

He takes a final drag of his cigarette and stubs it out on
Lucrezia Borgia; then he turns back to face the audience.

No matter how experienced or sophisticated you are,
you never see it coming, do you? I mean, when I stepped
into Murray's Club in Beak Street that wet and murky
Tuesday, why should it have been any different from the
dozens of other evenings I'd whiled away there?

SCENE TWO

As he's been speaking, the stage has transformed into
Murray's Club, a fairly seedy basement in Soho, relatively
empty tonight, with a scattering of men in suits, each at
his individual small table, some engaged in earnest
conversation with respectably dressed but over-made-up
young women. A small orchestra plays some jaunty late-
fifties-type melody. A Crooner sings energetically into a
microphone, standing in front of the tiny cabaret stage,
on which, at the back, are three girls wearing skimpy
grass skirts, topless, entirely motionless as the law
required, one arm up holding a pineapple, among them
an exceptionally pretty dark girl of sixteen with a mass
of copper hair: Christine Keeler; in front of them, half a
dozen Singer-Dancers, also grass-skirted and pineapple-
fronded, revealingly dressed but not topless, all spinning
hula-hoops. Stephen Ward moves confidently towards a
table at the side and takes a seat. It's the summer of 1959.

Crooner
   If you wanna make friends spin your body round and
      round

Girls
   Don't let your hoop fall to the ground

Crooner
   Everyone can do this grab yourself a little fun

Girls
   Follow me and see how it's done

Crooner
   Long as you got rhythm you got all that you need

Girls
   Don't be a party-pooper
   Be a super-duper hula-hooper
   Super-duper hula with me
   Make believe you're in Waikiki
   Underneath a coconut tree
   Don't be a party-pooper
   Be a super-duper hula-hooper

Crooner
   Put that hoop around you let your body start to sway

Girls
   Feel the real world slipping away

Crooner
   Come on all you hoopers – you feel great
   When you gyrate

Girls
   Perfect dance for losing some weight

Crooner
   Long as you got rhythm you got all that you need

Girls
Don't be a party-pooper
Be a super-duper hula-hooper
Lift your lazy butt off that chair
Hooping's like a breath of fresh air
They hoop in Paris and in Times Square
Everybody's hooping everywhere
Super-duper hula with me
Make believe you're in Waikiki
Underneath a coconut tree.
Don't be a party-pooper
Be a super-duper hula-hooper

A spirited hula-hoop dance as the orchestra builds to a frenzied climax. Scattered applause as they all skitter offstage. Light change. The orchestra segues into something smoochy and one or two couples take to the floor. The portly, perspiring, bespectacled, balding proprietor, Percival 'Pops' Murray, makes his way over to Ward's table.

Murray Dr Ward!

Ward Evening, Percy.

He nods to a dissipated, silver-haired dandy, Lord Boothby, who's leaving the club with a rough-looking dark-haired, blank-faced companion.

Evening, Bob.

Boothby Stephen.

Ward Who's that with Bob Boothby? Isn't that . . .?

Murray winks laboriously.

Murray Got it in one. His new friend Ronnie Kray.

Ward Heigh-ho.

He takes a seat: all the while, he's been expertly surveying the girls on stage.

7

Back row, the one on the left: new girl?

Murray Ah, Dr Ward, you do have an eye. That's Christine.

Ward She's a looker.

Murray Like to have a drink with her?

Ward Very much so.

Murray I'll send her out to you.

Ward I look forward to it.

Murray So you should, Doctor. Take it from me.

Ward Oh, Perce, you are a one.

Modestly accepting the compliment, Murray withdraws, smirking. A Waitress in a tutu brings Ward a Scotch on the rocks and he exchanges a pleasant word or two; then, with remarkable speed, Christine reappears in an evening gown a couple of sizes too large for her. She peers uncertainly at Ward, who rises to his feet and gestures to the empty chair beside him. He waits till she's seated before shaking her hand.

Ward Stephen Ward.

Christine Hello.

Ward Percy tells me your name is Christine.

Christine Christine Keeler, that's right.

Ward May I offer you a drink?

Christine Oh, champagne, please.

Ward turns easily to the Waitress, who still hovers in the vicinity.

Ward Lemonade, please, Noreen. And another Cutty Sark for me.

The Waitress sets off; only now does Ward settle next to Christine.

So where are you from?

Christine My parents have a place in Wraysbury.

Ward Oh, I know it. Not far from Runnymede.

Christine Staines, yes.

Ward Between Runnymede and Windsor.

Christine Sort of.

Ward Very handy for the airport.

Christine can't think what to say to this: she nods vaguely.

Always had a soft spot for Bucks.

Again, Christine is stumped.

Great friend of mine came from up round there: Vickie Martin.

Christine You knew Vickie Martin?

Ward Certainly did. You might even say I invented her.

Christine What do you mean?

Ward I gave her her name. Did you know her?

Christine I was at school with her little sister.

Ward Really?

Christine I remember seeing Vickie one day, driving past in a Rolls with her maharajah.

Ward Yes, I introduced them: I also told her not to marry him.

Christine What you do that for?

Ward He'd have whisked her off back to India. Vickie wouldn't have liked that very much. Though I suppose she might be alive now.

Christine is at last looking at him with some interest; he decides to press his advantage.

Would you care to dance?

He's on his feet, extending a hand to her, before she has time to answer. He leads her on to the tiny dance floor and whirls her round expertly.

We start out as strangers
The gods have brought us together
When I saw your face
I knew we'd be friends

When you get to know me
When we get to know each other
I'm certain that we will
Before the night ends

I'd like to know what makes you feel happy
What music makes you sad
All of our secrets slowly unravelled
Such good times to be had
We mustn't miss them

When you get to know me
When you get to know me better
Next time we meet

Christine
You won't get to know me
There ain't gonna be a next time
It's not what you think
I came for a drink

I hear the same thing over and over
Wasn't born yesterday

I have been through enough hoops this evening
I best be on my way
You must be joking

Still, happy to meet you
And better luck next time, Stephen
I'll say goodbye

She tries to move away from him as the music ends,
but he holds on to her hand.

Ward You remind me of Vickie.

Christine Do I?

Ward When she first arrived in London I found her in a
doorway in Oxford Street, sheltering from the rain. Not
very efficiently, she was soaked through.

Christine Why do I remind you of her?

Ward Your smile. Let me see you home.

Christine I'm on again in a minute.

Ward May I have your phone number?

Christine No, you may not.

Ward I hope you don't have a weakness for fast cars.

Christine Not specially.

Ward That's what did for Vickie. You know, the one that
killed her was her thirteenth car crash.

Christine Too good to be true, really, isn't it?

Ward What did you say your phone number was?

Christine checks a retort and relents, smiling.

Christine Regent 2150.

She slips away and disappears backstage. Ward turns
to the audience.

Ward
    I tried to phone her, she never answered
    Finally tracked her down
    Heard she spent weekends back home in Wraysbury
    Horrible little town

SCENE THREE

*A piece of waste land amidst gravel pits forms a corner of
an English version of a trailer park in Buckinghamshire
(now Berkshire) not far from the river. A patch of muddy
grass, worn away to earth in front of the converted
railway carriage sheathed in stained white cladding.
Clothes flap from a line.*

*The sound of a sports car drawing up: and presently
Ward appears, dressed informally (sports jacket, cavalry
twill, suede shoes and dark glasses). He squelches
gingerly across the patch of grass and knocks at the door
of the carriage, which opens to reveal Christine: she's
astonished and not best pleased to see him.*

Christine What are you doing here?

Ward You seemed to be too busy during the week to
come and see me: so I thought I'd come and see you.

Christine How'd you find out where I lived? Oh, never
mind, listen . . .

She leads him away from the door, lowering her voice.

My mum doesn't know about Murray's, she thinks I'm a
secretary, all right?

Ward Fine by me.

Christine I don't know, why'd you come?

Ward I want to get to know you better.

Whatever retort Christine is planning is interrupted by the door of the carriage opening. Christine's mother, Mrs Huish – a small, tousled woman, who's around forty, but looks older – appears in the doorway, her expression anxious and suspicious.

Mrs Huish Christine?

Christine Oh, Mum, this is Dr Ward.

Mrs Huish A doctor?

Ward moves easily over to her, hand outstretched; she takes it apprehensively.

Ward What a great pleasure to meet you, Mrs Keeler.

Mrs Huish I . . . remarried. I'm Mrs Huish.

Ward Mrs Huish.

Mrs Huish Mr Huish is out at the moment. At a business meeting.

Christine Down the pub.

Mrs Huish Christine.

Ward has his cigarette case out. He opens it and extends an arm.

Ward May I offer you a cigarette, Mrs Huish?

Mrs Huish Don't mind if I do.

She helps herself. Ward takes one for himself and lights them both.

Christine Don't I get one?

Ward You're too young to smoke.

He turns back to Mrs Huish.

Christine and I met at a . . . cocktail party in the week.

Mrs Huish She didn't say.

Ward looks around.

Ward I must say, what a marvellous place to live. All this . . . space.

Christine Might be better if we had electricity.

Ward What do you use, oil lamps?

Mrs Huish That's right.

Ward How romantic!

Christine Smelly, more like.

Ward makes an expansive gesture.

Ward
You're so very clever to have found this
The air is so much sweeter in the country
Afternoon tea
Under a tree
Close your eyes and you could be in Bridlington-on-Sea

Caravans are absolutely charming
Anywhere you go your home goes with you
You've so much freedom
The world's your oyster
The open road rolls by
What more could anybody ask for?
The woods the birds and the sky

Christine It's not a caravan, it's an old railway carriage.

Ward Well . . . same principle. I couldn't do without somewhere in the country.

He turns back to Mrs Huish.

Ward
I've a little cottage by the river
I like to go and stay there at the weekend
Warm breezes blow
Friends come and go
As the sun is setting the champagne begins to flow

Why don't I take Christine down and show her?
I could bring her back sometime this evening
It's a two-seater
Or I'd invite you
Maybe another day
Won't you give me your kind permission
To take Christine away?

You look far too young to have a daughter
Old enough to be a shorthand typist
She's so delightful
A credit to you
You've taught her grace and charm
Think of me as her guardian angel
I'll keep her safe from harm

He pauses, pleased with himself.

My cottage is at Cliveden. Just down the road, really.

Mrs Huish Go on, then, Christine, off you go.

Christine Why don't you go with him, if you're so keen?

Mrs Huish Now, come on, Christine, don't be silly.

Christine Well, I don't know if I want to go.

Mrs Huish Course you do.

Ward I'll bring you straight back if you don't like the look of it. Little spin'll do you good.

Christine pauses for a moment; then shrugs her shoulders.

Christine All right, then, suppose it won't do any harm.

Mrs Huish Course it won't.

Christine I'll just get my things.

She steps back into the carriage. Ward inclines his head to Mrs Huish.

Mrs Huish She's all over the place. She needs someone with a bit of sense to take her in hand and, like, guide her.

Ward I'll do what I can.

Mrs Huish She's very loyal, mind. She'll never let you down.

Ward I don't doubt it for a minute. Very good to meet you, Mrs Huish.

The door opens and Christine emerges with coat and handbag.

Christine Let's go if we're going.

Ward I don't think you'll regret it.

Christine You'd better let me be the judge of that.

Ward Oh, I will. That's where you young people are so lucky. You don't have to listen to anything you've been told; you can be the judge of everything.

Christine What do you mean?

Ward Things are changing, can't you smell it? People your age aren't going to put up with that old stuffy deferential world I was born into; and a good thing too.

Christine So you're a has-been?

Ward I am, that's right: but still hoping to be made an honorary young person.

SCENE FOUR

As Stephen Ward sings his song, he walks Christine into
a total change of scene: the exterior of his rented cottage
on the bank of the Thames at Cliveden. 'Cottage' is not
really the word for the substantial half-timbered house,
gabled, with a distinctive wooden first-floor balcony and
a twisting exterior wooden staircase. There's a tinkling
waterfall alongside the house, a rockery and flower beds
down by the river with irises and marigolds. Everything
is bathed in glorious late-afternoon sun.

By the time the song is ended, Christine is installed on
a chair facing Ward who is sketching her on an easel, his
chalks and black ink to hand.

Ward
You don't have to reach for heaven
Everything's right here
Times have changed and all the young are choosing
    freedom
You're the lucky generation
Why don't you aim high?
All you dream of can be found
This side of the sky

I've been waiting for the moment
When the walls come down
I believe life should be lived before it's over
On this golden summer evening
River flowing by
Paradise turns out to be
This side of the sky
There's another way to heaven
You don't have to die
If you're lucky you'll find heaven
This side of the sky

He stops drawing for a moment and looks across at her.

Are you warm enough?

Christine Yes, fine, thanks.

Ward We can go inside whenever you feel like it. Have a coffee.

Christine What, and you show me the bedroom?

Ward No, what makes you say that?

Christine They always say: 'Let me show you round,' and then they say: 'Just up there's the bedroom.'

Ward That's not what I'm like, little baby, you don't have to worry about me.

Christine Oh, do you play for the other team?

Ward No, no, nothing like that. I mean, I don't deny you're a beautiful girl, that's why I noticed you: but I never push myself on people. I just wanted to get to know you, that's all.

He hands her a cigarette, takes one himself, lights them both.

Christine How'd you find this place?

Ward Bill Astor, Lord Astor, one of my very best friends, he owns the big house up there. He likes to have me around. He has a bad back and I'm able to help him with it. I've been here about three years. Before that, it was lying empty for ages. He lets me have it for a pound a year.

Christine A pound a year?

Ward That's right.

Christine He hasn't got another one, has he? That bloody railway carriage is a guinea a week.

Ward Maybe you should come and live with me. In London.

Christine gapes at him. Silence.

Christine What are you talking about?

Ward Why not? I like you. I think we'd get on very well together. It's a bit cramped, but I'm looking round for somewhere a bit bigger.

Christine Well, you are a strange one.

Ward So they say.

Christine Aren't you married or something? They usually always are.

Ward I got married about ten years ago. Lasted all of six weeks. It's not for me.

Christine But you don't mind living with someone?

Ward Like a bit of company. And I have very interesting friends. I like meeting people. Bill's friends, for example. Everyone comes here: cabinet ministers, film stars, royalty. Lot of my guests here have fetched up with some life-altering new companions.

There's another way of thinking
I believe in love
I believe life should be lived before it's over
There's another way to heaven
No one has to die
Maybe heaven's always been
This side of the sky

William Waldorf, Third Viscount Astor ambles into view. He's in his early fifties, undistinguished-looking and hesitant in manner. He stands, listening and staring at Christine.

Christine
>Never seen a place so peaceful
>Like a fairy tale
>With no sign of any dragons in the forest
>I'm not used to being happy
>Makes me want to cry
>Never knew all this was waiting
>This side of the sky

Ward
>There's another way of living
>I believe in love
>I believe life must be lived before it's over
>
>There's another way to heaven
>No one has to die
>Maybe heaven's always been
>This side of the sky

Ward *and* **Christine**
>There's another way to heaven
>We don't have to die
>If we're lucky we find heaven
>This side of the sky

Ward Here's Bill, look.

Astor Who's this charming person?

Ward Christine Keeler – Viscount Astor.

Astor Bill, Bill. Lovely day. Want to come up for a swim, glass of champagne, that sort of thing?

Christine I don't have a swimming costume.

Astor We don't insist on them, you know. Or we could probably find one your size.

Ward Well, actually, I'm going to drive Christine home in a minute.

Astor Really? Seems a shame. Spot of dinner? Can't tempt you?

Ward I promised her mother I'd bring her back safe.

Astor Back's niggling me a bit.

Ward Won't be long. I'll do it soon as I get back.

Astor Oh, well. Hope you'll come again.

Ward She will, won't you, little baby?

Christine I shouldn't be surprised.

SCENE FIVE

Back at Murray's, the summer of the following year. On the little stage there's a reprise of the hula-hoop number. The row of motionless topless dancers contains a new performer: Mandy Rice-Davies, sixteen, a pert, attractive blonde.

Stephen Ward sits at his usual table for four (two empty seats) with a new acquaintance, a stocky Russian in naval uniform, Captain Eugene Ivanov, thirty-seven. They're watching the girls and drinking vodka. A nearby table seats three men, Ronnie and Reggie Kray, twins in their late twenties, and Lord 'Bob' Boothby. Further away is a chunky forty-year-old with a very young girl: he's Peter Rachman. In the background, Percy Murray weaves from table to table.

Girls
    Lift your lazy butt off that chair
    Hooping's like a breath of fresh air
    They hoop in Paris and in Times Square
    Everybody's hooping everywhere

    Super-duper-hula with me
    Make believe you're in Waikiki

Underneath a coconut tree
Don't be a party-pooper
Be a super-duper hula-hooper

Ward Eugene's not a Russian name, is it?

Ivanov Yevgeny.

Ward Ah.

Ivanov But when I am in West, I prefer to use Eugene.

Ward Fair enough.

Ivanov You call me Yevgeny in decadent London night club, I start to feel guilty. So I take name which can be pronounced by editor of *Daily Telegraph*.

The number comes to an end amidst a smattering of applause. The little stage empties.

And of course by young girls I may sometimes meet.

Ward They'll be out in a minute.

Ivanov I like that Christine with the dark red hair. Is it real or dye?

Ward It's not very difficult to find out.

Ivanov You know I'm very patriotic, I like a real Red.

Ward I can't say I've noticed that politics is the way to her heart.

Ivanov chuckles.

Speaking of politics, I must introduce you to my friend Jack Profumo, you know, the Minister for War.

Ivanov Oh, yes, that would be . . .

Ward Yes, just the sort of person you should get to know, things being as they are. Some sort of direct informal relationship, it's the only way to get round all this Cold War nonsense, don't you agree?

Ivanov Oh, yes, otherwise we are just prisoners of propaganda. You know . . . Ah, here come the girls.

Christine emerges from backstage in her evening gown, followed by Mandy. They make their way over to Ward's table. He stands to greet them, as does Ivanov.

Christine This is Mandy – Dr Stephen Ward.

Ward Lovely to meet you. This is my friend, Captain Eugene Ivanov.

Ivanov Please, ladies, sit down; you care for some vodka?

Christine We're supposed to order champagne.

Mandy But vodka would be nice.

Ivanov We will take both.

He waves to a Waitress as the girls sit; and Mandy turns her attention to Ward.

Mandy What sort of a doctor?

Ward Osteopath.

Mandy Does that mean massage and stuff? I could do with one of those.

Ward regards her indulgently for a moment. Ivanov pours vodka all round.

Ward
This is a world where there's all kinds of pressures
Where everyone's anxious and desperate for remedies
I use my hands to alleviate suffering
Slowly but surely I massage your cares away

Aches and pains and fractures and sprains
Manipulation – that's what I do
Lumps and knots and bruises and clots
Manipulation . . .

Mandy Doesn't sound very nice.

Ward It isn't.

Take a look at everyone here
Manipulation – that's what they do
I stretch limbs and they stretch the truth
Manipulation . . .

He smiles and lights a cigarette, not offering one to anybody. Christine sips at her vodka, makes a face.

Christine Never fancied Russia much.

Ivanov Oh, but this is terrible mistake. Russia is beautiful and home of greatest social experiment in history.

Christine Wouldn't suit me at all.

Ivanov So important we make friends, Russia and West. Otherwise . . .

He makes a sound and gesture signifying a massive explosion. Mandy isn't paying attention. She's momentarily intrigued by Ward.

Mandy What did you mean about manipulation?

Ward points at the nearby table, lowers his voice.

Ward You've heard of the Kray twins?

Mandy Sort of.

Ward Well, there they are. Two of the most powerful men in London.

Mandy But what do they do?

Ward They're gangsters. They have the police and the politicians in their pocket. Even Harold Macmillan, did he but know it.

Christine Who?

Ward Harold Macmillan, dear: the Prime Minister.

He draws on his cigarette, as Mandy discreetly stares at the twins.

There at that table the Kray twins are plotting
With Ronnie's new boyfriend Lord Boothby of
    Aberdeen
Also the lover of Lady Macmillan
Who we must assume is close to the Prime Minister

Ron and Reggie want something done
Bob Boothby breathes in Lady M's ear
Lady M sleeps with the PM
Manipulation – it's right here

He looks around the room.

Every table there's someone at it.

He points at a table in the back.

That chap in the Savile Row suit
That's Charlie Clore the entrepreneur
Built the Hilton mad about sex

Mandy
Didn't they just make him a sir?

Ward
Yes, but he was not at all pleased
Lord Clore's more what he had in mind

Mandy
Bloody hell the people you know
Don't suppose he's the marrying kind

Ward points over to Rachman's table.

Ward
That fat fellow – Rachman's his name
Owns two-thirds of Notting Hill Gate

He's the king of bedsitter-land
Manipulation . . .

I only try to manipulate bodies
I try to put people together and rescue them
I don't approve of exploiting the vulnerable
Lining your pockets from other men's weaknesses

Everywhere wherever you look
Manipulation rearing its head
London life there is no escape
Manipulation . . .

Mandy
I know what you're talking about
Manipulation just like you said
I spend every evening with men
Trying to sweet-talk me into bed

Ward, Mandy *and* **Christine**
Everywhere wherever you look
Manipulation rearing its head
London life there is no escape
Manipulation . . .

Everywhere wherever you look
Manipulation rearing its head
London life there is no escape
Manipulation till you're dead

Percy Murray has arrived at the table.

Murray Mandy!

Mandy Yes, Pops.

Murray Show me your hands.

Reluctantly, Mandy holds out her hands.

Your nail varnish is in a shocking state. Look, it's all cracked. That's a three-pound fine.

Peter Rachman has arrived at his elbow during this speech. He brings out a thick roll of banknotes secured by a rubber band and peels off a fiver. He speaks with a light Eastern European accent.

Rachman There you are, Perce, that should cover it.

Murray It doesn't really work like that, Peter.

Rachman Make an exception.

He stuffs the banknote into Murray's top pocket and turns pleasantly to Stephen.

Stephen, how are you?

Ward Peter: I was going to come over and say hello, ask your advice about something.

Rachman How can I help?

Ward Christine and I are a bit on top of one another in our current digs. Thought you might be able to show us something more spacious.

Rachman narrows his eyes, makes a lightning calculation.

Rachman Matter of fact, I think I have the very thing. I'm on my way there now, why don't you come along?

Ward I've got a patient any minute.

Rachman Oh well, I can show it to Christine then, see what she thinks.

Christine I'm on stage again in an hour.

Rachman I'll get you back; and Percy won't mind if you're a couple of minutes late, will you, Perce?

Murray Well, we try not to –

Rachman Yes, very good, we'll try not to as well.

He looks around genially.

And then later we can all have a drink at El Condor, what do you say?

Ivanov Where?

Rachman It's my club, I own it.

General murmurs of assent. Ward steps forward as the lights fade.

Ward
Well Peter Rachman did find us a bigger place
And just as well because Mandy moved in with us
I told them that I would not charge them rent
I just wanted them to share
Details of each love affair
They were quite a lively pair

SCENE SIX

Stephen Ward's small house in Wimpole Mews; the main room on the ground floor is a comfortable living room with well-used, fairly shabby furniture. The front door opens directly on to the Mews itself, which, for reasons which will become clear, is also visible. Christine, wearing one of Ward's old dressing gowns, sits on one of the sofas, smoking and nursing a mug of Nescafé. Mandy, fully dressed, is fixing herself a cup of tea in the little kitchen recess. Ward, smartly dressed in suit and tie, briefcase in hand, comes briskly down the stairs. Christine being more conveniently to hand, he bends to kiss her on the forehead.

Ward Morning, little baby; are you getting up or going to bed?

Christine Getting up.

There's a trace of indignation in her voice, which
amuses Ward; he delivers a quick peck on the cheek
to Mandy.

Ward All right, it's a fair question. Thought you might
have spent the night with old Sheikh Rattle and Roll.

Christine No, he didn't come in last night.

Ward Well, I have to love you and leave you. Duty calls
in the form of the royal arse of King Peter of Yugoslavia.

Mandy Oh, is it a nice one?

Ward I've seen worse. Catch you later, maybe.

And he's out of the front door and away down the
Mews. The door's hardly closed behind him when
Mandy puts her question.

Mandy Have you really never slept with Stephen?

Christine I've slept with him often enough; but we've
never had sex.

Mandy Why not? I thought he was pretty good news,
that weekend in Cliveden. Knows all the right things
to do.

Christine Haven't been back to him, though, have you?

Mandy No, but I haven't exactly ruled it out. And, I mean,
he's a good-looking man. Compared to Fatty Rachman.

Christine Hardly knew you were doing it with him. He
doesn't like to see your face, so you had to sit with your
back to him. Over in five minutes. He used to call it his
afternoon nap; and it was about as exciting.

Mandy That why you went off with the chauffeur?

Christine Well, he really did know what he was doing.

Mandy reflects for a moment.

Mandy What I want to know is, how can you live with a man and not do it?

Christine Makes a nice change, can't you see that?

Mandy Don't know, I suppose so.

Christine It's really . . . relaxing.

Mandy Yes, but what's in it for him, that's what I don't understand.

Christine decides to take the question seriously.

Christine
He sees something in me
Something no one else sees
He's like no other man that I've been with before
I feel safe around him
Nothing he says scares me
He knows so many girls I must have something more
He's happy just to chat

He makes me feel special
Treats me like a person
No man's done that
I had so many dreams
But none of them were this
My whole life has been changed
Without one single kiss

Mandy
What's the catch?
What is he after, must be something?

Christine
Well he's no spring chicken
Older than my father
The situation's wrong but somehow it feels right

Mandy
He must have some secrets

Christine
    Every man has secrets
    I'm not calling it love but some day I just might
    We're having so much fun
    He sees something in me
    I can't stop myself thinking
    That he's the one

Both girls are pensive for a moment, before Christine breaks the silence.

All the same, I miss Peter Rachman sometimes. There's something attractive about him, you know, in spite of his looks.

Mandy Is that right? He left me a note at the club last week. Asked me out.

Christine Oh, yes? You going?

Mandy Haven't decided.

Christine What about Saturday? You coming to that . . . dinner party thing Stephen was on about?

Mandy Will it be fun?

Christine So he says. He said last one he went to they served stuffed peacocks.

SCENE SEVEN

The drawing room of the flat in Hyde Park Square belonging to 'Hod' Dibben and Mariella Novotny: it's the delicate hiatus between the end of dinner and the start of the evening's orgy. Among the guests, many of whom are in various states of undress, are Ward, Christine and Mandy, as well as Bill Astor. Mariella Novotny, a twenty-year-old buxom blonde, is wearing a black corset with breasts

31

exposed, a garter-belt and black stockings; her husband
Hod – a grizzled fifty-five-year-old antique dealer and
nightclub owner with sideburns and a leather suit –
watches her fondly as she makes the rounds. Coffee is
being served from a silver tray by a man, who is naked
except for a small, frilly apron, a bow tie and a black
mask covering his face and tied at the back. Ward is
talking to Hod and Astor.

All
> Ten years back
> Life was grim
> Men were dull
> Girls were prim
> Fogs were thick
> Food was bland
> Sex was all
> In the hand
>
> Our idea
> Of obscene
> Early night
> Ovaltine
> That's all gone
> As you see
> We're all rich
> Love is free
>
> You've never had it so good
> You've never had it so often
> Go and do what you never could
> A brand new brother and sisterhood
> You've never had it so good

Ward By the way, did you see Joseph Kennedy had a massive stroke?

Hod No.

Astor He's a great friend of my mother's. Used to come round all the time during the war. They had quite a lot in common.

Ward Oh, yes, what?

Astor Both frightfully keen on Hitler.

Hod Mariella had a dalliance with the President, didn't you, dear?

Mariella Yes, at the Hampshire House on Central Park. Good-looking fellow.

Ward Really, what was he like?

Mariella Bit preoccupied. Still, he gave me a hundred dollars. Worked out about seventy-five dollars a minute.

Men
Do you like
S and M?

Women
I don't mind
One of them

Men
Here you can
Have it off

All
With some old
English toff

Christine *and* **Mandy**
Who is that
In the mask?

All
They won't say
So don't ask

Women
> Could be some
> Royal duke

Girl
> Possibly
> King Farouk

All
> You've never had it so good
> You've never had it so often
> Chelsea's buzzing like Hollywood
> In Mayfair it's well understood
> You've never had it so good

The Man in the Mask pauses in front of Mariella.

Man in the Mask I hope everything is to your satisfaction, mistress.

Mariella Why are you interrupting? Did I ask you to stick your oar in?

Man in the Mask No, mistress, sorry, mistress.

Mariella And where's the white sugar?

Man in the Mask I thought people preferred brown with their coffee.

Mariella You thought, you thought: who asked you to think?

Man in the Mask Nobody, mistress.

Mariella Go in the kitchen. Bill will be in to chastise you in a minute, won't you, Bill?

Astor Whatever you say, Mariella.

Man in the Mask Oh, thank you, mistress.

Mariella You won't thank me when Bill's finished with you.

The Man in the Mask scurries off; and Mariella taps her cup with a spoon for silence.

I'm blowing the whistle for the kick-off! Here we go! It's everybody's lucky day!

A kind of courtly dance begins, as the orgy gets under way.

All
Pair off
It's time to pair off
The whistle goes and they're off

Now's the time for you to show your mettle
Last one with their clothes off boils the kettle
Spanking
I'm all for spanking
Which stranger am I thanking?

You'll feel so good once you've got all your clothes off
You'll find you are ready for anything
I'm saying
One thing's for sure you are not going to doze off
It's down on your knees but no praying

Stroke me
Somebody stroke me
Punish me, prod and poke me
Smother me in strawberries and lick me
Bring out your embroidery and prick me
Use me
Come on and use me
Don't hang about abuse me

Just wave goodbye to those dull inhibitions
You just have to be ready for everything
Get started!
It's time to try those ambitious positions
The ones that scare off the faint-hearted

You've never had it so good
You've never had it so often
Go and do what you never could
A brand new brother and sisterhood
You've never had it so good
You've never had it so good!

Total abandon.

SCENE EIGHT

*The El Rio Café in Notting Hill, a murky basement with
a largely black clientele. Ward and Christine appear and
rather tentatively sit at a corner table. Ward looks
around, fascinated. There's a small band playing at the
back of the room; and the singer, a small, bald man with
a neat goatee, Aloysius 'Lucky' Gordon, thirty-one,
launches into his number.*

Lucky
She is a black-hearted woman
Don't be fooled her smile is smooth as peanut butter
She's just a black-hearted woman
If I don't leave I'm going to end up in some gutter
She steals my cash while I'm sleepin'
And it's me who does the washin' and the sweepin'

She is a black-hearted woman
Come a long way from those dark and dirty ghettos
Just a black-hearted woman
She's the devil in a pair of black stilettos
In time my sad heart will shatter
But when we make love that doesn't seem to matter

She's a black-hearted woman
She will drink my last drop of Jamaica rum
She's just a black-hearted woman

She would toss my car keys in the river for fun
In time my sad heart will shatter
But when we make love that doesn't seem to matter

Scattered applause.

Ward The singer's the man to ask, apparently. I think you'd better do it, little baby. He'll think I'm a plain-clothes man.

Christine You mean just go up and . . .?

Ward Absolutely.

Christine obediently rises and heads over towards Lucky Gordon. Ward takes out his sketchbook, opens it on the table and begins sketching. Christine reaches Lucky, who greets her with an easy smile.

Lucky Hi, baby, anything I can do for you?

Christine I'm looking for something.

Lucky You found it, baby; I'll show you later on tonight.

Christine I was looking for some . . . grass.

Lucky You come to the right lawn, baby. How much you need?

Christine Erm, how does it come?

Lucky A pound, ten shill.

Christine fumbles in her bag, comes out with a brown banknote.

Christine I'll take the ten shillings.

Lucky You got it.

He makes no move, beyond trousering the ten-shilling note.

Christine You don't have a sister by any chance, do you?

Lucky I got plenty of sisters, can help you any way you like.

Christine It's just that my . . .

She indicates Ward, who's watching with the greatest interest.

. . . brother, well, he's always wanted to get to know a black girl.

Lucky I can get him two or three if he has the funds.

Christine I think one'll do to start off.

Lucky What's your name, baby?

Christine Christine.

Lucky Well, I'm Lucky Gordon and this is your lucky day. You and me's going to be the best of friends, Christine. I'll go get your stuff.

He turns and slips out of the room: Christine makes her way back to Ward, giving him the thumbs-up as she approaches. She sits down at the table.

Christine I got ten bob's worth.

Ward Where is it?

Christine He's bringing it over.

Ward Oh.

Christine And he says he's got a sister you can try out.

Ward Ah.

Christine Never let it be said I don't look out for you.

A tall, slightly older black man, Johnny Edgecombe, thirty-four, materialises at Ward's table.

Edgecombe Hi, folks, I'm Johnny the Edge.

Ward Evening. Join us.

Edgecombe pulls over a chair, addresses Christine.

Edgecombe Couldn't help seeing you conversing with Gordon. Said to myself, there's a chick with class, what's she doing talking to that little rat?

Christine Oh, well . . .

Ward Business matter.

Edgecombe Well, I don't know what the . . .

He's interrupted by the arrival of Lucky.

Lucky Johnny!

Edgecombe How's tricks, Lucky?

Lucky hands a twist of paper to Christine.

Lucky There you are, darlin'.

Christine Thanks.

Lucky Wish I could come smoke it with you.

He turns back to Edgecombe.

I hear there's a couple of boys out looking for you, Johnny.

Edgecombe That so? Friends of yours, maybe?

He turns his attention to Christine.

You don't want to come to this dump no more, darlin': I got a much better place up the hill, a nice little shebeen.

Lucky Go drinking in there, you be blind in six weeks.

Edgecombe Aloysius, my son, you the living proof that ain't true.

Lucky Johnny's the kind of guy steals your watch one day, tries to sell it back to you the next.

Ward has closed his sketchbook and now rises to his feet.

Ward I think we'd better be off.

Lucky Not going already?

Ward Afraid we have to.

Lucky Leave me your number, man, I'm going to be picking out one of my sisters. A good one.

Ward Well, thank you.

Edgecombe Handle with care.

Ward, nevertheless, scribbles his number on a scrap of paper and hands it to Lucky.

Lucky Johnny will pay for your drinks.

Ward We didn't have any drinks.

Lucky That's OK: Johnny don't have no money.

Ward Come along, little baby. Nice talking to you, gentlemen.

He holds out a hand to Christine, who rises to her feet and takes it, apparently with some reluctance. Ward walks her into the next scene.

Cliveden on a summer weekend was as if *Who's Who* had just come to life; dukes and ministers and presidents – Bill invited the world and his wife.

SCENE NINE

Cliveden: the area by the pool, which glimmers, just offstage, in the shadow of the immense house. Ward and Christine sit with Eugene Ivanov, drinking champagne on a summer's night.

Ivanov

> Mother Russia
> You are always with me
> Mother Russia
> Weeping for your children
> Hold me in your mighty arms
>
> Mother Russia
> I can hear your music
> Playing softly
> In my heart forever
> And those melodies still play
> Even when I'm far away
> So far away from Russia
> You are always in my soul
> In my soul forever

*He sings the song partly in Russian, partly in English.
By the time he finishes, he's in tears, which he wipes
away with his sleeve. He gestures up at the great
house.*

In Russia, of course, we have great houses, also, palaces
like this. But in Russia they belong to all the people, not
just few lucky capitalists.

Ward More champagne?

Ivanov Thank you. I'm sorry for caviar this evening; was
not the best quality.

Christine Never really liked it. Gives me heartburn,
something terrible.

Ivanov Makes me homesick, even when is not good.

Ward You'd really rather be there than here?

Ivanov Better in Russia than anywhere. Is true, is
beautiful here. But how much longer can it last?

Ward See us out, I shouldn't wonder.

Ivanov You know what Premier Khrushchev says this week to your Ambassador in Moscow?

Ward No, what?

Ivanov He told him with only six bombs he can destroy whole of United Kingdom.

Christine Well, that wasn't very nice.

Ivanov You don't understand, Christine, we are walking blindfold on tightrope across Niagara Falls.

Christine What are you talking about?

Ivanov We are driving fast towards edge of cliff. Next war will be the last.

> How can people
> Understand what's happening?
> Propaganda
> Everything's distorted
> By your politicians' lies

Ward
> And *your* politicians' lies

> Mother Russia
> Stupid situation
> There's no reason
> We should fight each other
> Must be something we can do

Ward *and* **Ivanov**
> Those bloody lies will kill us
> We are doing what we can
> To stop the bombs from falling

Christine What can you do exactly?

Ward I'm directly in touch with MI5 and Eugene reports back to his people. The Foreign Office knows it can use us to send unofficial messages. It's something we call back-channels.

Christine But you think we're all doomed?

Ward It's quite possible. Which means, I think, Eugene, that it's our duty to have as good a time as we possibly can, wouldn't you say?

Ivanov You are so right, Stephen.

> This could be our very last day on earth
> Let's have fun while we can
> Let's go wild and party for all we're worth
> Come let's sing and let's dance while we still can
>
> By dawn all of us could go up in smoke
> So let's live while we can
> Let's get drunk and what you say go for broke
> We are alive so let's live while we still can

He starts tearing off his shirt.

First thing, I take a swim.

Christine It's so hot, wouldn't that be lovely?

Ward Well, go on then.

Christine Haven't got a costume.

Ward So what, nobody minds.

By this time, Ivanov, who is wearing swimming trunks under his trousers, is rushing offstage; a mighty splash announces his arrival in the pool. Christine undresses and hurries after him. Sounds of aquatic pleasure. Ward pinches one of Ivanov's cigarettes and lights it, settles back luxuriously.

Presently, from the other direction, sounds of approaching conversation. Bill Astor appears, in a dinner jacket, with his guest, John ('Jack') Profumo, the Minister for War. As they arrive, Ward, moving

*like lightning, gathers up Christine's clothes and hides
them under the table; then he picks up a nearby towel.*

Astor I think you know Stephen Ward, don't you, Jack?

Profumo We have met, yes.

Ward Mr Profumo.

*They shake hands; but Profumo is much more
interested in what's going on in the pool. He moves
in that direction, where shrieks and splashes can be
heard; just as he arrives close to the edge of the pool,
a naked Christine, running away from Ivanov, looking
over her shoulder, crashes right into him.*

Profumo Well, well, well.

*A certain amount of chaos ensues. Christine manages
to grab the towel from Ward after a brief, fierce tug-
of-war, but then Astor and Profumo chase her, trying
to get the towel back from her, which Profumo
eventually succeeds in doing – just as a number of
other guests arrive, including Astor's young and
pregnant wife Bronwen, Ayub Khan, the President of
Pakistan, and Profumo's wife, the beautiful and
elegant Valerie Hobson. This has the effect of bringing
an abrupt end to the horseplay. Valerie is the first to
assess the situation; she calmly takes the towel away
from Profumo and hands it to Christine.*

Valerie I think this must be what you're looking for, my
dear.

Christine Thank you.

*Hiatus. Then Bill Astor steps forward, slightly out of
breath, to fill the vacuum.*

Astor Let's see now: President Ayub Khan, Jack Profumo,
Valerie Profumo, Captain Ivanov, Stephen Ward, Bronwen
you all know, and, um, Christine, Christine Keeler.

A good deal of hand-shaking ensues, but Christine judges it prudent to withdraw.

Christine If you'll excuse me . . .

She gathers her towel around her and slips away. Profumo, eagle-eyed, has spotted her clothes under the table, bends, gathers them up and murmurs to Ward.

Profumo These hers?

Ward Yes.

Profumo She'll be needing them, I shouldn't wonder.

Ward Not urgently.

Profumo All the same . . .

He sets off in the same direction as Christine, a purposeful glint in his eye. Meanwhile Astor, anxious to steer the party in a different direction, leans towards Ayub Khan.

Astor You a keen gardener, President Ayub?

Ayub Khan Insofar as our native soil permits, which is not that far, I regret to say. I learned to marvel at English gardens, when I was at Sandhurst.

Astor Come and look at our rose garden, then. It's really quite fun.

SCENE TEN

Mid-afternoon: the main bedroom in Stephen Ward's house in Wimpole Mews. Christine lies in bed between the sheets. Jack Profumo is almost dressed, sitting on the side of the bed doing up his shoelaces. He leans over to give Christine an affectionate kiss, surreptitiously checking his watch as he does so.

Profumo Well, that was wonderful, darling.

Christine yawns luxuriously.

I wish I didn't have to tear myself away.

Christine Do you?

Profumo I'm afraid I have to go and vote in the House.

Christine Can't they do without you for once?

Profumo Well, strictly speaking, they probably could. But my absence would be rather frowned on: they've put out a three-line whip.

Christine Kinky.

Profumo Yes, indeed.

Christine What are you voting on?

Profumo Er . . . bit complicated to explain.

Aware of the feebleness of this response, he tries a little harder.

It's to do with defence procurement.

Christine Oh.

Profumo Even more kinky.

He makes an effort to change the subject.

I wish we didn't have to meet in Stephen's house. I keep expecting him to burst in on us. Makes me nervous.

Christine Your house was much more fun.

Profumo Yes, but Valerie's so rarely away.

He's doing up his tie; pauses in mid-knot.

I've been thinking . . .

Christine What?

Profumo Couldn't I find you somewhere else to live?

Christine sits up, frowning.

Christine I like living here.

Profumo goes to sit on the edge of the bed.

Profumo
We should get a little flat
Somewhere we could call our own
We deserve a hideaway
Some place we can be alone

I know someone I can phone
He'll start working right away
He knows Knightsbridge back to front
I'll get on to him today

He will find a pied-à-terre
In a quiet private square
A romantic secret lair
To continue our aff—

Christine interrupts him.

Christine
Thanks but no I'm eighteen
There's a world out there
That I've never seen
I'm too young
I can't let you lock me away
Why do men
Always feel
They can tie you down
With this mistress spiel?
I don't want
To become a walking cliché

Freedom means the world to me
I'm really sorry, Jack,
I just have to be free

Profumo
> You'll still be free as a bird
> I would never cramp your style
> You could go your own sweet way
> I'd come by once in a while

Christine
> I'm sure you mean what you say
> I'm really sorry, Jack
> It never works that way

She gets out of bed, throws her arms around him and pecks him on the cheek. They make an entirely unsuitable couple – her naked, him in his pinstripes.

Got time for a cup of tea before you go?

SCENE ELEVEN

Stephen Ward steps forward to address the audience.

Ward And so, after a quite short relationship, exciting for him and pretty run-of-the-mill for Christine, they parted company – with nothing to give anyone the slightest hint that the two of them had just enjoyed one of the most notorious affairs of the century. When the Cuban missile crisis came along, Eugene and I tried to do what we could, and with my MI5 contacts, I think we really were able to make a small contribution towards heading off World War Three. We could have done with having instant access to Jack Profumo; but by that time, Christine had left him very far behind and moved into her own flat.

> Funny how things can turn out
> Things that seemed unimportant
> Suddenly make big headlines everywhere

Christine longed for excitement
Mandy moved in with Rachman
I was looking for someone else to share

Mandy got a commercial
Had to be shot in New York
Both of them set sail on the SS *France*

Christine seduced the waiter
Soon moved on to the captain
You only had to give her half a chance

Their trip was a disaster
TV ad was cancelled
They went to Fire Island for a rest

They thought they'd get stampeded when they started
  to undress
But all they got was blisters from the sun
There were all these handsome boys there they were
  hoping to impress

And they thought they had it made
When they saw the cavalcade
Of male beauty on parade
They felt certain they'd get laid

Christine *and* **Mandy**
  USA
  What a dump

  Rows and rows of poufs that you couldn't hump
  Couldn't wait to get back to W8

Christine
  Take a pill
  Notting Hill
  Smoke some pot
  Then sit back and chill
  Take a brother home and show him the way

Christine *and* **Mandy**
> Freedom means the world to me
> I'll wake up where I like
> I just have to be free

Ward
> Christine got hooked on black lovers
> Didn't cross her mind they might not like each other
> But if you have two wild lovers
> Take care one doesn't find out about his brother
> When Lucky found she was cheating
> He decided he'd give Edgecombe a beating

> *Behind him, a choreographed knife-fight erupts*
> *between Lucky and Edgecombe, Christine vainly*
> *trying to stop it. It ends with Edgecombe razor-*
> *slashing Lucky's cheek and leaving him bleeding*
> *copiously.*

After that, Christine had to go into hiding. Meanwhile,
Mandy's boyfriend, Peter Rachman, sex with whom,
Christine had told me, was like going to the dentist –
'And I,' she said, 'was the toothpaste' – surprised us all
by finally doing something not for profit: he keeled over
and dropped dead. Poor Mandy was genuinely upset: she
took an overdose and had to have her stomach pumped.
And what with one thing and another, by the end of the
year, Christine and Mandy were both back living with me.

SCENE TWELVE

Back at Ward's house in Wimpole Mews, shortly before
Christmas 1962. Christine relaxes, smoking a joint;
Mandy, pale beneath her elaborate make-up, sits in front
of a mirror listlessly taking out her rollers and dropping
them into their container, occasionally sipping from a
tumbler of whisky.

Mandy

When you found me lying there
I wish you'd have let me die
All that I keep thinking is
Peter's dead so why aren't I?

I adored that little man
Funny bald and overweight
I still can't believe he's gone

Christine

Cheer up, love
Don't be blue
There'll be other men
To look after you
You're too young
You can't let yourself fade away

If you'd died
Bet your arse
He'd have set up home
With some Mayfair brass
Thought of you
Maybe once or twice every day

Time that you were moving on
Now nineteen sixty-two
Is almost dead and gone

Nineteen sixty-three
We'll be fancy free
Yeah yeah
We can start again
A better class of men
Find a whole new scene

Mandy

Let's write to Steve McQueen

Christine *and* **Mandy**

Yeah yeah

Mandy
   Isn't he the best?

Christine
   Bet he's like all the rest

Christine *and* **Mandy**
   No more bad times
   Last year was a bitch
   We must find new ways
   Of scratching that itch

   No more the fool
   Who follows her heart
   It's almost New Year
   Let's make a new start

   Nineteen sixty-three
   We'll be fancy free
   Yeah yeah

Christine
   We will hit the heights

Christine *and* **Mandy**
   Have some outrageous nights

Christine
   We will raise our game

Mandy
   And grab our share of fame

Christine *and* **Mandy**
   Yeah yeah

Christine
   Have a little spree

Mandy
   With President Kennedy

Christine *and* **Mandy**
No more old farts
With middle-aged wives

Christine
And no more wide boys
Running our lives

Mandy
No more posh gits
And no more rough trade
We just use our heads

Christine *and* **Mandy**
And we've got it made

Mandy
Modelling jobs
In Paris and Rome
We're flying first-class
All the way home

Christine
Shooting a test
For some full-page ad
The cover of *Vogue*

Mandy
That wouldn't be bad

Christine *and* **Mandy**
Nineteen sixty-three
We'll be on TV
Yeah yeah

Mandy
We will make our names

Christine
Twelve months of fun and games

Mandy
Wear a low-cut dress

Christine
Our pictures in the press

Christine *and* **Mandy**
Yeah yeah

Mandy
Chauffeured limousine

Christine
From *Playboy* magazine

Christine *and* **Mandy**
No more bad times
Last year was a bitch
We must find new ways
Of scratching that itch

No more the fool
Who follows her heart
It's almost New Year
Let's make a new start

No more bad times
Last year was a bitch
We must find new ways
Of scratching that itch

No more the fool
Who follows her heart
It's almost New Year
Let's make a new start

Mandy And no more posh orgies.

Christine *and* **Mandy**
We've never had it so good
We've never had it so often
We're gonna do what we never could . . .

*As the song moves towards its climax, Johnny
Edgecombe appears outside in the Mews. He saunters
towards the front door and pauses there, clearly
hearing the girls as the song approaches its joyous
conclusion. He leans against the doorbell, cutting them
off in mid-flow. Inside the house, Christine and Mandy
look at each other, shocked. Then, as Edgecombe rings
the doorbell a second time, Christine starts to move
towards the door. Mandy hisses at her, stopping her in
her tracks.*

Mandy Wait!

*Holding up a hand, she crosses cautiously to the
window and peeks out; she shrinks back immediately,
whispering to Christine.*

It's Johnny.

Christine What?

*Before she can react any further, Edgecombe bangs
furiously on the door.*

Edgecombe Christine! I know you're in there!

Christine For God's sake, don't tell him I'm here!

*Edgecombe rings the doorbell again. The girls
exchange another frightened glance. Then, gingerly,
Mandy edges back to the window and opens it.*

Mandy Johnny!

Edgecombe Where's Christine? I need to talk to her.

Mandy She's . . . at the hairdresser's, Johnny. Having her
hair done.

Edgecombe No, she ain't: she's there.

Mandy She's not, Johnny, I promise you.

Edgecombe Fucking liar! I know you been seeing Lucky again, ain't you? I know you have.

Mandy Oh, my God, Christine, he's got a gun!

Edgecombe points the gun at her. She ducks back from the window, terrified. Another blast on the doorbell. Christine takes a deep breath. She crosses boldly to the window. But before she can speak, Edgecombe fires at her, twice.

Both girls scream and Christine throws herself to the floor. She and Mandy try to scramble under one of the sofas, which is however too close to the floor to be able to accommodate them, though in their panic they continue to try to squeeze under it. Meanwhile, Edgecombe fires two more shots into the door.

Jesus, Christine, now what?

Blackout.

Act Two

It's New Year's Eve, 1962. The curtain rises on the same scene; only now the Mews is jammed with reporters and photographers, who have obviously been camped there for some time. Christine is in the process of completing the packing of one of two suitcases; her expression is mutinous and angry. Mandy is off to one side, doing something in the kitchen. Stephen Ward is watching Christine, shaking his head ruefully. He turns to the audience.

Ward Christine hadn't seen Jack Profumo for over a year and Eugene had been recalled to Moscow; so it never crossed my mind that the whole business would come tumbling out of the closet. I couldn't take it seriously. When some journalist asked me if I thought she might have spoken to Jack about the deployment of nuclear warheads to West Germany, I told him it was highly unlikely, because her mouth was generally full. I utterly underestimated the investigative diligence of the *News of the World*.

He steps forward to confront Christine.

Christine I don't know why you're doing this, Stephen!

Ward
Christine you don't seem to understand
I had a very successful practice here
Till your black friend got his pistol out
Shot my reputation full of holes
Christine, I can't let this go on
Losing patients hand over fist
Every front page covered this mess

Christine

    Can't you move to another address?

Ward

    I'm afraid you're going to have to go
    You must have friends up in Notting Hill
    I'll see you when this has quietened down
    But for now you have to pack your bags

Christine

    Don't exaggerate
    This will die away
    All the dirt
    And all the gossip
    Tell me you'll let me stay!

    You saw something in me
    Something no one else saw
    How can you throw me out?
    Tonight is New Year's Eve

    You thought I was special
    Why can't you forgive me?
    I just don't understand
    Why I should have to leave

    Why can't you look again
    And see something in me?
    You have never hurt me
    Like other men

    She lowers her head, miserable.

It's not my fault, Stephen.

Ward Before you dump your insanely jealous boyfriend, you lend him a revolver and give him my address, how could it possibly be your fault?

    Christine's expression hardens.

Christine You're going to regret this.

Mandy
Leave the man alone
He's been through enough
Christine
We'll find somewhere else
Till this dies down

Take a look outside
All that noisy mob
Christine
Let's just slip away
And find some other town

Christine
Why don't you mind your own fucking business?

Mandy
You've sort of made it our business
Why don't you give him a breather?
Let him get back on his feet

Christine turns away from her and glares at Ward.

Christine You'll be hearing from me.

Ward I don't doubt it.

Christine takes some time to check her appearance in the hall mirror; then she picks up her suitcases. Ward opens the door for her, and she disappears into a scrummage of shouting reporters and flashbulbs. The gang of press follows her down the Mews and away.

SCENE TWO

An office in the News of the World *building. Christine sits, out of her depth and a little uncomfortable, as three Journalists circle her, notepads in hand. A reel-to-reel tape recorder is in operation, its reels slowly revolving on a table set up near Christine's chair. Christine aims for (but fails to achieve) a tone of jaunty indifference.*

Christine I'm not sure I know what it is you gentlemen are after.

First Journalist
Give us something juicy

Second Journalist
What was Jack like in bed?

Third Journalist
If it's really juicy it could make you rich

First Journalist
Make it nice and fruity
Tell us what Astor said
How did he persuade you when he got the itch?

Second Journalist
Who came in the front as
You slipped Jack out the back?
Any chance it could have been a Russian spy?

Third Journalist
Did you mention missiles
In the sack with old Jack?
Was Ivanov chatty when he stroked your thigh?

Christine Ivanov?

Third Journalist You heard me.

Christine
Hang about
what's your game?
Where did you
Get that name?

First Journalist What's it matter, love?

Christine I thought I was here to talk about Johnny Edgecombe.

Second Journalist You're here to talk about whatever we want you to talk about.

Third Journalist Such as whether you discussed matters of national security when you were in bed with the Minister for War.

Christine
When he gave
Way to lust
Missiles weren't
Much discussed

Third Journalist
And Ivanov?

Christine
Eugene was a very big vodka man
He'd have ten for the road
And then things would never go quite to plan
I don't think that he ever shot his load

First Journalist Whoa there!

Second Journalist That's not what we want to hear.

Christine Well, it only happened once at the very most: and then we were both so drunk, neither of us could really remember what we'd done.

Silence. The Journalists look at each other.

Surely we owe your readers the truth, don't we?

First Journalist
Don't be bloody stupid

Second Journalist
Where's the fun reading that?

Third Journalist
We need something juicy for papers to sell

Never mind what happened
They want tit they want tat
He may not have fucked you, Christine, what the hell?

Second Journalist
We owe it to our readers
All the news fit to print
That is our proud credo on the street of shame

First Journalist
Play your cards right, darling
Or you could end up skint
Do you want the gutter or a life of fame?

Christine
You wanted my story
You promised me glory
Never told me I was going to have to lie

First Journalist
You don't understand
It's twenty-four grand
News of the World readers set their sights quite high

Second Journalist
Without something juicy
This ain't worth thirty bob

Third Journalist
We'll do all the writing it's a piece of cake

All Journalists
Tell us something juicy
Come on love do your job

First Journalist
Orgies

Second Journalist
Niggers

Third Journalist
  Warheads

All Journalists
  Real news for Christ's sake!

  Tell us something juicy
  Come on love do your job
  Orgies
  Niggers
  Warheads
  Real news for Christ's sake!
  Orgies
  Niggers
  Warheads
  Real news for Christ's sake!

First Journalist See, we just need to throw the poor old punter a bit of red meat on a Sunday morning.

Second Journalist Just leave it to us and you'll find you're sitting on a goldmine.

Third Journalist If you'll pardon the expression.

First Journalist One thing all this proves.

Second *and* **Third Journalists**   What?

First Journalist Life is better under the Conservatives.

  Raucous laughter.

Christine Well, I do have this letter you might be interested in. From Mr Profumo.

  Lights out on the Journalists. Stephen Ward appears.

Ward I could see Christine was getting ready to kiss and tell; so I got Jack Profumo to meet me in the Dorchester.

A quiet corner in the cavernous foyer of the Dorchester
Hotel. Stephen Ward sits with John Profumo: there's a
cup of coffee in front of Ward, nothing in front of
Profumo. It's early March 1963.

Profumo Christine Keeler? Remind me.

Ward Oh, come on, don't do this. You know perfectly
well who she is. If she's slipped your mind, ask the head
of MI5. Or George Wigg and his Labour colleagues, they
seem very well informed.

Profumo Wigg just hates being outsmarted every time
I'm at the dispatch box. But, yes, of course I remember
Christine. How is she?

Ward This is really why I wanted to see you: to warn
you. She's on the rampage. She's trying to sell her story
to the newspapers. Bill Astor – he's been a great support,
I really don't know what I'd do without him – anyway,
he and I managed to head her off by threatening to sue
the paper and saying we were sure you'd do the same.

Profumo Well, I'd have to.

Ward Quite: but she's such an unpredictable dimwit, no
one knows where she's going to pop up next.

Profumo So what do you suggest?

Ward I don't know, really: I used to have some influence
on her, but she's furious with me, ever since I told her to
move out. I need hardly have bothered; the police are still
round most days asking to interview my patients: most of
whom are now consequently my ex-patients. Isn't there
someone we could get to lean on her, just to get her to
shut up? I don't see why I should have to take the rap for
your bit of fun.

Profumo gives this a moment's thought; it's obvious he doesn't like Ward's tone.

Profumo As a matter of fact, I've already spoken to MI5. Thought we might be able to slap a D-Notice on the press. But they won't play ball: Hollis just wants to wash his hands of the whole thing.

Ward But I couldn't have been more co-operative. I told MI5 everything I knew about Ivanov. He and I offered to act as back-channels all the way through the missile crisis. I think I was very helpful.

Profumo doesn't bother to conceal his expression of polite scepticism.

Profumo Yes, well, be that as it may, I'm afraid there's only so much one can do to circumvent the occasionally inconvenient principles of free speech. I'll speak to my lawyers, you speak to yours and maybe they can come up with something.

Silence. Profumo shakes his head.

It never crossed my mind she could be capable of causing so much trouble.

SCENE FOUR

The drawing room of the Profumos' house in Chester Terrace, Regent's Park, at two in the morning. Profumo, buttoning up his clean shirt, is trying to focus, still bleary-eyed from sleep. Present are the Chief Whip, Brigadier Martin Redmayne, the Solicitor-General, Sir Peter Rawlinson and the Attorney-General, Sir John Hobson. Valerie Hobson (no relation) comes in and hands Profumo a cup of black coffee. She's in a beautiful dressing gown.

Valerie Drink that down, darling.

As he does so, she turns to the others, all charm.

Are you sure I can't get you gentlemen anything?

Gruff murmurs of refusal from all three.

You must forgive Jack, he's taken a sleeping pill, that's why he's so woozy. He couldn't get to sleep for the noise all those ghastly photographers were making. Our man was obliged to trade blows with one of them.

Redmayne Dreadful.

Profumo Are you sure this is absolutely necessary?

Hobson You heard what that bounder Wigg said.

Rawlinson And the other two: Mrs Castle was the worst of all.

Profumo No, I missed the whole thing. I was enjoying an exemplary Gevrey-Chambertin.

Redmayne Bill Deedes was there throughout: he said the insinuations simply can't go unanswered.

Rawlinson And Iain Macleod says we have to make the statement in the morning or the weekend press will eat us for breakfast.

Profumo turns to Valerie.

Profumo Do you think you could find me some cufflinks, darling?

Valerie Of course.

She leaves the room; Hobson waits until she's left before he puts his question.

Hobson Iain said, before we all get into this up to the armpits, there's one basic question that has to be answered . . .

He hesitates.

Profumo Which is?

Hobson He said: 'The question is, did Jack fuck her?'

Silence.

Redmayne Well, did you?

Profumo Of course not!

Valerie returns with a pair of gold cufflinks, which she hands to Profumo.

Thank you, Pidge.

He starts trying to thread the cufflinks as the three visitors gather around him.

Redmayne
This is frightfully important and we have to get it right
And nip these filthy rumours in the bud

Rawlinson
We must get this statement drafted if it takes all
　　bloody night

Redmayne
Things will not look quite so black
If we go on the attack

Hobson
But you'd better speak up, Jack
If there's info that we lack

Profumo is having a terrible time with his cufflinks. Valerie steps in to take over.

Valerie Let me, darling.

Profumo
It's absurd – pack of lies
Something Labour's just trying on for size

I think we have to take a very strong line
Let's find out who's to blame
I'll sue anyone who maligns my name
We all know Wigg's a sanctimonious swine

And when we do find out, rest assured I shall definitely
take legal action.

*Valerie has finished with his cufflinks; he puts his arm
around her.*

Thank you, my darling.

My name means the world to me
I promise you there's been
No impropriety

SCENE FIVE

*Spotlit, isolated, Profumo makes his statement to a
packed and muttering House of Commons. He looks
utterly calm and composed.*

Profumo . . . I would like to take this opportunity of
making a personal statement about these matters: I last
saw Miss Keeler in December 1961 and I have not seen
her since. I have no idea where she is now. My wife and
I first met Miss Keeler at a house party in July 1961 at
Cliveden. Among a number of people there was Dr
Stephen Ward, whom we already knew slightly, and a Mr
Ivanov, who was an attaché at the Russian Embassy. The
only other occasion that my wife or I met Mr Ivanov was
for a moment at the official reception for Major Gagarin
at the Soviet Embassy. My wife and I had a standing
invitation to visit Dr Ward. Between July and December,
1961 I met Miss Keeler on about half a dozen occasions
at Dr Ward's flat, when I called to see him and his friends.
Miss Keeler and I were on friendly terms. There was no

impropriety whatsoever in my acquaintanceship with Miss Keeler. Mr Speaker, I shall not hesitate to issue writs for libel and slander if scandalous allegations are made or reported outside the House.

He sits down to a tumultuous reception, mostly cheers from the Conservative benches.

SCENE SIX

The Home Secretary's private quarters in the Home Office. The Home Secretary himself, Henry Brooke, a large, florid man with a slightly baffled air, sits behind his desk facing the head of MI5, Roger Hollis. Both men look up as the Commissioner of the Metropolitan Police, Sir Joseph Simpson, is shown into the room.

Brooke Ah, Commissioner, thank you for coming so promptly.

Simpson Home Secretary – Roger.

He shakes hands with Hollis and sits on a hard upright chair rather than one of the deep leather armchairs Hollis has gone for.

Brooke I asked Roger here to brief me on MI5's dealings with this wretched Stephen Ward; I thought it would be good to have your views as well.

Hollis I was explaining to the Home Secretary that Ward has absolutely no grasp whatsoever of the real world. He imagined he had his finger on the pulse, but he never gave us a single piece of information we didn't know already. He's a fantasist.

Simpson What's the objective, Home Secretary?

Brooke To put it bluntly, I want to know if we can close him down.

This is a terribly serious matter
The Government's future is in jeopardy
This fellow Ward went and threatened Profumo
He can't keep his mouth shut

Hollis

How best can we deal with him?

Brooke

Shift the blame and blacken his name
Let's find a way to put him inside
Shift the blame put him in the frame
And keep the whole damn thing

All

Classified

Hollis

Now that Ivanov's been called back to Russia
There isn't a chance we could get Ward for espionage
And by the way he was working on our behalf
Writing useless reports on Ivanov's proclivities

All

So no charge for espionage
There must be something else we can do
It's high time we thought of a crime
Manipulation – nothing new

Simpson

Hollis is right there's no chance of conviction
Perhaps we should focus on sexual behaviour
Immoral earnings now that might be possible
Some of those girls must have slipped him a bob
  or two

Brooke

That's the one, can you get it done?

Simpson

It won't be easy but we can try

Brooke
What I need is you to succeed
So we can all kiss Ward goodbye

All
We can all kiss Ward goodbye
We all know the way it should go
Manipulation – that's the technique

Brooke
Now forget that we ever met

Hollis
This conversation must not leak

All
This conversation will not leak
This conversation will not leak
This conversation will not leak!

SCENE SEVEN

*Commissioner Simpson walks into a corridor in
Marylebone Police Station and buttonholes Chief Inspector
Samuel Herbert, a grim, unsmiling figure with an abrupt
manner. The corridor abuts a bleak interview room
where Christine Keeler waits, squirming uncomfortably
on her chair, supervised by Detective Sergeant John
Diggs, a plain-clothes man with a pipe, younger than
Herbert and kindlier-seeming.*

Simpson Ah, Chief Inspector, glad I caught you.
Everything all right?

Herbert I'm just going in to interrogate Keeler.

Simpson I wanted to let you know, this is a more than
usually sensitive case. The Home Secretary's taking a
particular interest.

Herbert You mean he wants a conviction, sir?

Simpson He requires one.

Herbert Tricky thing is, sir, I've had a word with my colleagues in Vice, and no one's heard so much as a squeak about Ward, all these years.

Simpson So what's your plan?

Herbert We're going to have to rely on the girls. We'll get a few of them in and come down heavy on them. We should be able to get what we need.

Simpson Good, good. If all goes according to plan, I don't think you'll find the Home Secretary unappreciative.

Herbert Say no more, sir.

Simpson slips away and Herbert steps into the interview room. In the next part of the scene, by some ingenious device, the interviewees, sitting in hard chairs facing their interrogators and a blank wall, are seen one at a time, but succeed each other instantaneously. Diggs stands up as Herbert enters the room.

Diggs There you are, Chief. I was saying to Christine here, she must be getting used to us by now. Old friends, almost.

Christine Yes.

Herbert is staring at Christine, his expression stony.

Herbert Where'd you get that bruise?

Christine Well, I . . .

Herbert Don't tell me you walked into a door; or I may have to walk you into another one.

He chuckles mirthlessly.

Diggs Perhaps it was one of your darkie friends. That it?

Christine No, I . . .

Diggs We know he was round to see you last night.
Lucky.

Herbert And we know he's partial to a spot of GBH.

Christine No, it wasn't . . .

Diggs See, you'd be helping us out, Christine, if you
happened to remember that it was Lucky done that to you.

Herbert And we know you have a very helpful disposition.

Christine I . . . suppose it might have been Lucky.

Diggs That's my girl.

Herbert We'll come back to that. Just remember . . .

Herbert *and* **Diggs**
    You could be in trouble
    If you don't help us out
    You could be in prison for a good long time

Diggs And now we want to talk about your favourite
doctor.

Herbert
    How long's he been pimping?
    What's that freak all about?
    We know he's a criminal but what's the crime?

Christine
    I don't know
    What you mean
    Stephen is
    Squeaky clean

    I told you
    All along
    Stephen's done
    Nothing wrong

Diggs

We know he's a pervert
We've got him bang to rights
He's been on our radar for a year or two

Herbert

Don't be stupid, Christine
All of those steamy nights
Somebody was paying to get into you

*The spotlight snaps out on Christine; now, it's Mandy
Rice-Davies sitting in front of the policemen.*

Diggs

How're you coping, Mandy?
Got a nice roomy cell?
We can get you out if you co-operate

Herbert

We can leave you in here
If you refuse to tell
It's all up to you love to decide your fate

Mandy

First I get arrested at Heathrow
Then I'm carted off to Holloway
Then my bail is set two thousand quid
You'd think that I killed Doris Day

Furthermore they shaved my pubic hair
Do they do that for a parking fine?
All the prison warders are bull dykes
It's not an encouraging sign

'Cause my payments are behind
On a TV I can't find
I've a little question for you, John
Tell me what the fuck's going on?

Diggs
Let's get down to business
We need Ward facing court
You can give us evidence you know you can

Mandy You mean all this is about Stephen? Is that what you're saying?

Herbert
This Dr Savundra
Wouldn't have left you short
What was Ward's percentage from this wealthy man?

Mandy disappears, as the spotlight shifts to Lucky Gordon.

Diggs Well, Miss Keeler quite clearly stated that you assaulted her.

Herbert You bashed her, didn't you, Lucky, old son.

Lucky I have done in the past, I won't tell you a lie, but this time absolutely not. I swear I'm innocent.

Diggs
Now we can help you out, Lucky
But we're gonna need a little information

Herbert
We're after Stephen Ward, sunshine
We know what he's done we want verification

Diggs *and* **Herbert**
If you won't talk then believe us
We will definitely send you down for grievous

Diggs
We're after him for procuring
He provides young girls for toffs and politicians

Herbert
You must have known what he's up to
Did you help him to fulfil his dark ambitions?

Diggs *and* **Herbert**
You've got one chance can't you see man
Testify and you walk out of here a free man

Lucky faces them down, his expression defiant.

Lucky You're not going to get me to grass anyone up,
I don't do that.

Diggs Your mate Edgecombe's just gone down for seven
years, that what you want?

Lucky Go fuck yourselves.

Herbert Bad decision, Lucky. See you in court.

Lucky disappears: to be replaced by Vickie Barrett.

Vickie
Yes Ward was my client
I went round twice a week
He liked me to whip him with a bamboo cane

Diggs
That is useful, Vickie
But it needs a little tweak
Say it was his friends you had to entertain

Vickie
It's not true
Why should I
Say that when
It's a lie?

Herbert
'Cause otherwise
You will soon see
See what a bastard
I can be

He twists her ear.

Vickie
Ouch you're hurting
All right I give in
I'll say anything
You like I can't win

Herbert
If I say lie
Lie you will
Or goodbye
Notting Hill

And Vickie gives way to the far more robust figure of Ronna Ricardo, a dark girl with dyed red hair, who stares contemptuously back at the two policemen.

Diggs *and* **Herbert**
All you have to say is
That you slept with Ward's chums
And slipped him some money, Ronna, then you're
   through

Ronna
Tossers
You pair of tossers
Half-witted double-crossers
Can't trust you as far as I can throw you
I've got something here I'd like to show you

She surges to her feet, lifts her skirt and lowers her underwear, to reveal, stencilled across her stomach, the words ALL COPPERS ARE BASTARDS. *She points at the words, spelling them out.*

All coppers are bastards.

Herbert shakes his head, unimpressed.

Herbert Sit down.

The quiet menace in his voice slightly takes the wind out of Ronna's sails. She sinks down.

You're just not
Very smart
Even for
An old tart

Diggs
How is your
Baby boy?
Bet he's your
Pride and joy

Herbert
How's your little sister?
It must be crowded there
She's still on probation your delinquent sis
How'd you like to see her
Taken back into care?
And we could take your baby it's a piece of piss

By now, Ronna is subdued. Tears begin to trickle down her face.

Ronna You wouldn't take my baby.

Herbert You give us a hard time, Ronna, and you just watch us.

Ronna disappears and the spotlight falls on an acutely uncomfortable Bill Astor. The policemen's manner is transformed into something deferential, bordering on obsequious.

Herbert
Good of you to find the time, Your Lordship
This should not detain us very long, sir
I hope we can
Speak man to man
It's got very messy since the shit has hit the fan

Diggs
We need to know the women you have slept with
Their names and how much money you have paid them
Did Ward supply them?
Was he rewarded?
Did you pay Mandy's rent?

Diggs *and* **Herbert**
We hate to put these questions to you
But how much have you spent?

Astor is looking at them aghast, his mouth open.

SCENE EIGHT

An early summer evening on the private terrace of a suite at the Hotel Cipriani in Venice. Valerie Hobson sits, nursing a Bellini; there's another on the small table between the two chairs. John Profumo can be heard offstage, winding up a telephone call in the suite, from which he presently emerges.

Profumo (*offstage, on the telephone*) Yes, of course. I'll see you then.

Valerie Everything all right, darling?

Profumo Well, not really; that was Dilhorne. He wants to move our Thursday meeting to Wednesday.

Valerie Oh, you poor thing, what a bore. That means we'll have to change our flight.

Profumo Yes.

By this time, he's taken his seat and picked up his Bellini. Distractedly, he crunches a couple of salted almonds. Pregnant silence, which Valerie, looking concerned now, eventually breaks.

Valerie Is something the matter?

Profumo I don't know how to say this in any other way, darling: the fact is, I did have an affair with that wretched girl.

Valerie maintains an unruffled calm: she takes a sip of her Bellini.

Valerie I see.

Profumo I'm sure you suspected as much.

Valerie I didn't, actually. I believed you implicitly.

Profumo I'm sorry, darling. I can't tell you how terrible I feel about it.

Valerie I can't deny I'm extremely disappointed in you.

Profumo I'm extremely disappointed in myself.

Silence.

Valerie What are you planning to do?

Profumo Well . . .

Valerie You're going to have to own up and tell the truth, aren't you?

Profumo Well, if I do, it means I'll be forced to resign.

Valerie Then, yes: resign.

Profumo There's going to be the most appalling stink.

Valerie I know: but you can't go on like this, can you? Better to go back and put the best face on it you can.

Profumo considers for a moment, evidently anguished; finally, he sighs deeply.

Profumo You're quite right. You're always right.

Valerie Not always: but I think I am this time.

Profumo We'd better leave in the morning. And we should probably take the train, the airport will be swarming with press.

Valerie Yes.

Profumo I'm so sorry, darling, if you only knew how sorry I am.

He reaches out for her hand, but she snatches it away.

Valerie It's not enough, is it?

Profumo No.

Suddenly, Valerie's calm disappears: she's furious.

Valerie How could you? Taking all those stupid risks: and for *that*!

Profumo It was so long ago. I never thought she would . . .

Valerie I don't know the history of it and I don't want to. It's the lies I can't stand, the betrayal, lying to everyone, lying to *me* over and over again.

Profumo I know, you're right, I know.

Valerie What did you think you were doing?

He doesn't know how to answer the question and rises unsteadily to his feet.

Profumo I'd better go and start making the arrangements.

He steps back into the suite. Valerie sits for a moment, lost in thought.

Valerie
My life is far from over
Time to think about me
I could live a life without you
But what kind of life would that be?

Part of me is saying I should go
Maybe that's what I should do
But I will not be leaving
I'm hopeless when it comes to you

You can't stay with him that's what they say
And some days their words ring true
But those are fleeting feelings
I'm hopeless when it comes to you

You're bruised but you're not broken
There'll be no more lies
We'll go on together
Dry each other's eyes

This will make us stronger than before
Sometimes that's what pain can do
How could I think of leaving?
I'm hopeless when it comes to you

Profumo returns, tentative. Valerie reaches out a hand to him.

It's eight years now since I took your name. I was proud of it then and I always will be. These eight years have been the best years of my life.

Profumo Thank you, my angel. I don't know what I could ever have done to deserve you.

He lifts her hand to his lips and kisses it.

Valerie
We're bruised but we're not broken
There'll be no more lies
We'll grow strong together
Dry each other's eyes

This will make us closer than before
Sometimes that's what pain can do
How could I think of leaving?

I'm hopeless when it comes to you
I'm hopeless when it comes to you

SCENE NINE

Stephen Ward's Mews house; he's letting in Bill Astor.

Ward Bill, come in, come in! I was so pleased to hear from you.

Astor makes some half-hearted sound of assent as he steps into the main room.

And very touched that you should have phoned more or less the minute you landed. I knew I could count on you.

Astor Well . . .

Ward You've no idea how ghastly it's been. The police have been let loose on me. I think they're determined I get all the blame; and since Profumo resigned, it's got even worse. I honestly think they're about to arrest me.

Astor What for?

Ward I don't know, some ludicrous morals charge. How they think they're going to make it stick, it's a mystery. Anyway, I know all it needs is a word from you in the right ear and they'll drop the whole investigation. But don't let me rattle on. You said you needed to see me urgently . . .

Astor Yes.

Ward Well, here I am.

Agonised pause.

Astor The thing is, Stephen . . . the keys to the cottage at Cliveden . . .

Ward Yes?

Astor I wonder if you could let me have them back.

Stunned silence.

Ward You want the keys back?

Astor Well, you know, Stephen . . . what with one thing and another . . .

Ward Yes, I see. Well, of course.

He turns around, almost giddy for a moment.

I think they're in the kitchen.

Astor Not now, I don't need them this minute.

Ward Oh. . .

Astor In fact, I think the best thing would be if you write me a letter saying under the circumstances you're sorry but you think you'll have to vacate the property, etc., etc. . . .

Ward A letter.

Astor Yes, I don't want it to seem as if I'm pushing you out, wouldn't look good, I'm sure you understand.

Ward I'm beginning to.

Astor I'm so sorry about this, Stephen, you know, Bronwen rather insists on it.

Ward Yes, yes, of course, I can see that.

Astor I had a word with my chum, the Bishop of Buckingham, this was very much his advice.

Ward I do understand.

Astor I knew you would.

He lets out a groan of relief.

Gosh, I'm glad that's over with. Been absolutely dreading it.

Ward says nothing. His expression is bleak.

I hope you're wrong about them arresting you, but if it does come to a trial, you won't let them call me, will you?

Ward No, I won't, I promise.

Astor Could be frightfully awkward.

Ward Please don't worry about it.

Astor Thanks, that's a real weight off my mind.

Silence. Ward, for once in his life, can't think of what to say next.

Course, if you need a bit of a sub towards your legal costs, just give a shout, anything I can do.

Ward Well, thank you, Bill.

Astor Not at all. Goes without saying.

He leaves the house. Ward, on his own, sinks into a chair. He looks devastated. He sits in silence, as we watch the approach of Chief Inspector Herbert and Detective Sergeant Diggs, accompanied by a couple of uniformed constables. Ward starts when he hears the knock on the door. He gets up, crosses to the door and opens it; then steps back to let the policemen in.

Diggs Stephen Ward?

Ward Yes.

Diggs I am placing you under arrest on charges of procuring and living on the earnings of prostitution.

Ward Oh, my God, how dreadful.

Diggs I must warn you that anything you say may be taken down and used in evidence against you.

By now, Ward has succeeded in pulling himself together.

Ward It's all right. You won't find anyone to come forward and say it's true.

Herbert Would you mind coming with us, sir?

Ward leaves with the policemen and they lead him towards the entrance to the Old Bailey, where a baying crowd is gathered, waiting for the trial to begin.

Crowd
You disgusting pervert
Stephen Ward filthy scum
See what happens to you when you're in the nick

What an evil bastard
You're as bent as they come
You'll be going down for years you sad old prick

Crowd 1
Stephen Ward arrested on immoral earnings charge
Prime Minister expected to resign
Profumo – Profumo
Now the Tory Party quakes
He's a pimp, a bloody pimp
He's a pimp, a bloody pimp
He's a pimp, a bloody pimp
Innocent my arse, is he innocent my arse
He's a sex-mad dog

Crowd 2
Stephen Ward arrested on immoral earnings charge
Morally repugnant, orgy probe
Ward arrested on immoral earnings charge
He's a pimp, he's a pimp, a bloody pimp
He's a pimp, a bloody pimp
He's a pimp, a bloody pimp
Country reached an all-time low
Pimp, a bloody sex-mad dog

Crowd 3

Arrested
Stephen Ward arrested
Prime Minister expected to resign
Dirty doctor faces orgy charge
He's a pimp, he's a bloody pimp, a bloody pimp
He's a pimp, a bloody pimp
He's a pimp, a bloody pimp
He's a sex-mad dog
He's a sex-mad dog

Crowd 4

Resign! – Resign!
Charge Profumo – Profumo
Sex-mad, sex-mad dog
He's a sex-mad dog
He's a sex-mad dog

*Ward disappears, and first Christine, then Mandy run
the gauntlet of the crowd, bunched up on the pavement,
yelling and jeering at Christine, arriving in her
mustard-coloured suit, cape and high-heeled shoes.*

Crowd

Here comes Christine Keeler
Drops her drawers for the rich
All you need's a fiver for a first-class shag

Here comes Christine Keeler
What a tart what a bitch
Hanging's too good for you, you disgusting slag

*Christine manages to get through, pale and shaken;
she's followed by Mandy in a short, grey sleeveless
dress and a hat shaped like rose petals. She receives the
attention of the crowd with a good deal more aplomb
than Christine.*

Crowd
Mandy
It's little Mandy
You'd make a bishop randy
Bet she's up to all kinds of malarkey
Least she never did it with a darkie

Mandy passes through the crowd and disappears.

SCENE TEN

*Court No. 1 at the Old Bailey. The principals are in
place: in the dock, which is surprisingly large and roomy,
is Stephen Ward; to one side is his defence counsel, James
Burge, a good-humoured and jovial-looking man; to the
other, the Crown Prosecutor, Mervyn Griffith-Jones, a
tall, dapper, square-jawed man with a severe expression;
and in the centre, the Judge, Sir Archie Marshall, a small,
tubby man in his sixties with a beady eye and an
unimpressive manner. By a trick similar to that employed
in the police interview room, the witnesses are enabled to
replace one another instantaneously; and now Christine
is in the witness-box and Mr Griffith-Jones is on his feet,
cross-examining her.*

Griffith-Jones When you were living at Comeragh Road,
did the defendant introduce you to other people?

Christine A few of his friends, yes.

Griffith-Jones Did you have sexual intercourse with any
of these persons?

Christine I can't really remember.

The Judge leans forward to intervene.

Judge Well, think, Miss Keeler.

Silence. She appears to be thinking.

Christine I can't remember.

Griffith-Jones People he introduced to you?

Silence. Christine thinks some more.

Christine Maybe a couple.

Griffith-Jones Were you paid for it?

Christine Oh, no.

Griffith-Jones Did you receive money from *anybody* while you were living at Comeragh Road?

Christine Mr James Eylan, maybe.

Griffith-Jones You were having intercourse with him?

Christine Yes.

Griffith-Jones Who introduced you to him?

Christine I met him myself. I would like to say that I am not a prostitute and never have been.

Judge We'll come to that in a moment.

Griffith-Jones Did Ward ever say anything to you about going to Mr Eylan?

Christine No.

Griffith-Jones The Russian, Ivanov, did he give you anything?

Christine No.

Griffith-Jones You told the preliminary hearing that you had had intercourse with a man called Charles, who had given you £50.

Christine Yes.

Griffith-Jones How did you meet this Charles?

Christine Dr Ward introduced us.

Griffith-Jones On receiving the £50, after intercourse, did you speak to Ward about it?

Christine I can't remember.

Griffith-Jones What did you do with the £50?

Christine I used some of it to repay a loan to Dr Ward.

Griffith-Jones's eyes light up in a discreet sort of way.

Griffith-Jones Can you tell the jury roughly what proportion of the money you received you handed over to the defendant?

Christine Oh, I usually owed him far more than I ever made: and I only gave him half of that.

Griffith-Jones frowns; and Christine is replaced in the witness-box by Mandy.

Griffith-Jones How did you pay for the rent of the flat at Comeragh Road?

Mandy I didn't pay for it.

Griffith-Jones How was it paid?

Mandy By cheque.

Griffith-Jones Whose cheque?

Mandy Lord Astor's cheque.

Griffith-Jones Who introduced you to Lord Astor?

Mandy Stephen: the defendant.

Griffith-Jones Did you have intercourse with Lord Astor?

Mandy Not then: two years later.

Griffith-Jones Lord Astor has denied ever having intercourse with you.

Mandy Well, he would, wouldn't he?

Laughter in the court; the Judge looks angry.

Griffith-Jones Were you having intercourse with other men at the time?

Mandy Peter Rachman.

Griffith-Jones Anyone else?

Mandy Douglas Fairbanks, Jr.

Griffith-Jones Anyone else?

Mandy My boyfriend.

Griffith-Jones Were you paid by these men?

Mandy No, except for Peter Rachman. He kept me.

Griffith-Jones When you had intercourse with Lord Astor, was Ward present at the flat?

Mandy Once. It was quite normal for him to be in the flat.

Griffith-Jones It was normal for Ward to be in the flat when you were having sexual intercourse with other men?

Mandy Oh, yes; it's quite normal, isn't it? What's wrong with it?

Judge When you were in the flat, were there occasions when you were handed money?

Mandy Several times. I'd give him money. Just a couple of pounds or so.

Griffith-Jones Apart from this money and your modelling fees, had you any other money coming in?

Mandy Only what Stephen gave me.

For a moment, Griffith-Jones is perplexed: then he tries a different tack.

Griffith-Jones Did you say at the preliminary hearing that you hoped Dr Ward would be acquitted?

Mandy Yes, sir. He doesn't deserve this. You might as well arrest every bachelor in London!

More laughter. The Judge shouts 'Silence!' Mandy disappears, to be replaced by Ronna Ricardo.

Griffith-Jones Earlier this year, you visited Ward at his flat, is that so?

Ronna Yes. With my boyfriend and another girl.

Griffith-Jones Did you have intercourse with anybody on that occasion?

Ronna Yes, I did.

Griffith-Jones With whom?

Ronna My boyfriend.

Griffith-Jones What did the other girl do?

Silence. Finally, Ronna reluctantly answers, her voice quiet and subdued.

Ronna She was with Stephen.

Griffith-Jones In the other bedroom?

Ronna tries to speak but can't: eventually, she shakes her head.

In the same room?

Silence.

Were all four of you taking part together?

Ronna nods, biting her lip. Murmurs in the court.

Judge I want to hear what happened in that room. Was there anything *beyond* sexual intercourse?

Ronna shakes her head, mystified.

Griffith-Jones How many times did you go to Ward's flat?

Ronna Once.

Griffith-Jones Once? Are you quite certain?

Ronna Once. Never more than once.

The Judge leans forward and attempts a patronising tone.

Judge We at the Bar are men of the world – and we know that people do not go into a lounge four-in-hand and have sexual intercourse unless there exists between them some special relationship.

Ronna We never set out to have sexual intercourse . . .

The Judge sits back, baffled; and Griffith-Jones takes up the cudgels again.

Griffith-Jones In your statement to the police, you say: 'After Christmas, Stephen introduced me to a man, but I can't remember his name.' Did he do that?

Ronna No.

Griffith-Jones frowns; but decides to persist.

Griffith-Jones 'I had sex with this man in the flat. He gave me a "pony".' Did you say that?

Ronna No.

Griffith-Jones How did this come to be in the statement you signed, unless you said it?

Silence. Ronna bites her lip again and looks on the brink of tears.

Judge Are you suggesting the police just . . . put these words into your mouth?

Ronna Yes.

Griffith-Jones You must realise to have these words put into your mouth and written down as yours is a very wicked thing to do. Did you never complain?

Ronna looks at him for a moment, as if he's an idiot.

Ronna Who could I complain to?

Griffith-Jones The jury will want to know how you came to sign this statement as true, if it is all invention put in by the police.

Ronna I was kept so long at the police station, I was ready to sign anything. I didn't want to sign that statement.

Griffith-Jones Then why did you sign it?

Ronna I didn't want my little sister Dorothy to go to remand home.

Griffith-Jones How would this stop your sister from going to remand home?

Ronna And Chief Inspector Herbert told me they would take my baby away as well.

Silence, as the court digests this bombshell; then Ronna adds, quietly:

I thought if I helped them, they'd help me.

A recess. The Judge and Mr Griffith-Jones convene, their manner anxious. Ward and Mr Burge, on the other hand, are modestly elated.

Ward I don't mind admitting, when I heard Christine and Mandy were going to be witnesses for the prosecution, I was a bit shaken, but they came through, didn't they? They're not such bad girls.

Couldn't be going better
All their plans are backfiring
Needn't have been so anxious after all

Burge
Cautiously optimistic
Too soon to throw a party
But it looks like they are heading for a fall

Ward
Griffith-Jones
Pompous arse
He is like a man in a Whitehall farce
Trousers round his ankles caught in the act

Soon I'm going to be free
We'll go back to my place
The drinks will be on me

The focus switches to the Judge and Mr Griffith-Jones.

Judge Well, Mervyn, this is going to need a miracle.

Griffith-Jones I think we still have one or two tricks up our sleeve.

Judge
Not one witness said what they needed to
Clearly your whole case is in jeopardy
Ronna Ricardo was really quite damaging
The police should have scared her a bit more
    convincingly

Griffith-Jones
All of that's just an unfortunate hiccup
I'll bet my shirt on this girl Vickie Barrett

Judge There is one other problem: Lucky Gordon's jury has quashed his conviction.

Griffith-Jones Ah, yes, that is quite a problem. Did they say that Keeler's evidence was fiction?

Judge No, but that's what they were implying; he was convicted by her perjury, her lying.

Griffith-Jones
Never mind
I shall say
He'd be free
Anyway

He was un-
Fairly tried
Not because
Keeler lied

I'll go on
The attack
After all
Fellow's black

Vickie Barrett she is our ace
I've coached her

Judge
Coached her?

Griffith-Jones
She knows what to say
Once the jury looks at her face
I'm sure that we can call it a day

Police gave her a pretty good scare
Manipulation works every time
All I need is Ward standing there
Give me the man and I'll find the crime

The court reassembles; now, it's Vickie Barrett in the witness-box.

Will you tell the court how you came to meet the defendant?

Vickie I met him in Oxford Street. I was just by Oxford Circus tube station, when he drove up in a white Jaguar. He asked me if I'd like to go to a party.

Griffith-Jones What did you say?

Vickie I said: 'I don't like parties.'

Griffith-Jones What else did he say?

Vickie He said he would give me some money if I stayed for two hours. We drove to his flat. On the way he told me what he wanted me to do.

Griffith-Jones What was that?

Vickie He said there was a man at the flat who wanted to go with a girl and he said the man would give him the money.

Griffith-Jones What was he going to do with the money?

Vickie He said if I visited him two or three times a week, he would save the money and I could live in a flat.

Griffith-Jones On arrival did he take you into the flat?

Vickie Yes.

Griffith-Jones What did he say?

Vickie He said the man was waiting in the bedroom. He gave me a contraceptive and told me to go in the room and strip; and he said he would make coffee.

Griffith-Jones Was there a man in the bedroom?

Vickie Yes.

Griffith-Jones Dressed in anything?

Vickie No.

Griffith-Jones Did you have sexual intercourse with him?

Vickie Yes.

Griffith-Jones When you were having your coffee with the defendant, was anything said about money?

Vickie Yes. Ward said he had already received it.

Griffith-Jones Did you agree to him keeping it for you?

Vickie Yes.

Griffith-Jones You went round to the flat again the following Friday, is that correct?

Vickie Yes.

Griffith-Jones Was there a man there?

Vickie Yes.

Griffith-Jones Was he in the bed?

Vickie He was in the bedroom in bed.

Griffith-Jones Were you given a contraceptive?

Vickie No. When I went into the bedroom, there was a cane on the bed.

Griffith-Jones Did you use it?

Vickie Yes.

Griffith-Jones Did you have ordinary sexual intercourse?

Vickie No.

The Judge, who has been hanging on every word, now intervenes.

Judge During this time, how were you dressed?

Vickie In underwear and high-heeled shoes.

Griffith-Jones Where did you find the high-heeled shoes?

Vickie They were my own.

Griffith-Jones Was Ward still in the sitting room when you returned?

Vickie Yes, with the coffee.

Griffith-Jones Was anything said about the money to be paid for whipping the man?

Vickie No.

Griffith-Jones Nothing about a 'monkey' to be paid for each visit?

Vickie No.

Griffith-Jones glowers at her.

Yes.

Griffith-Jones With your knowledge of the trade, Miss Barrett – or rather, the profession – what would be the normal payment for services such as you rendered?

Vickie Five pounds in the flat.

Griffith-Jones And for the whipping, what is the market price?

Vickie One pound a stroke.

Vickie disappears; and James Burge rises to his feet.

Burge Ladies and gentlemen of the jury . . .

His manner is entirely candid and straightforward.

Was this life of Ward's led for fun or profit? That is the key to this case. Was he conducting a business? There's a very, very wide gap between a man with an artistic temperament and with obviously high sexual proclivities leading a dissolute life and saying he has committed these offences.

He shakes his head and speaks with great conviction.

Can you really imagine this man has been living on the earnings of prostitution? On a fair and impartial view, I will ask you to say these charges have not been made out and find him not guilty.

He resumes his seat, to be replaced by the towering figure of Mr Griffith-Jones, who launches straight into the attack.

Griffith-Jones
Here's a monster of depravity
Who went hunting fresh and tender game
Picked up two young semi-prostitutes
Promised them a first-hand taste of fame

If so minded one might well infer
Profit was his motive and his goal
When he first set foot in Murray's Club
Seeking victims that he could control

So-called Doctor Ward went to endless lengths
Making sure Keeler was succumbing to his influence
Even went as far as visiting
Her little people in Staines to reassure them

If so minded one could well conclude
This is evil in its purest shape
Preying on the weak and vulnerable
Once the trap closed there was no escape

You have heard what the accused made Vickie Barrett
   do
Offering her to all his friends – hard to believe but true
Holding back the money that she thought he would
   repay
Clearly money from immoral earnings you may say

Ward, who has been becoming increasingly agitated during this diatribe, can't prevent himself from shouting out.

Ward No!

Judge This is not the first time you have interrupted and I will take action if you do it again.

Ward I'm sorry, My Lord. It's a great strain.

Griffith-Jones's eyes light up and he seizes his opportunity.

Griffith-Jones Of course it's a great strain for a guilty man to hear the truth at last.

He allows himself a small triumphant smirk.

If so minded one might well assume
This defendant should not be set free
To resume his filthy way of life
Of seduction and debauchery

Judge Members of the jury –

The Judge begins in a mild, neutral manner.

You have here in front of you a man of many parts
A successful osteopath and patron of the arts
A highly distinguished healer
A true artist not a fake
These are very hard decisions
You are called to make

Suddenly, his tone changes: he turns to look at Ward, his expression fierce, and delivers a ferocious, almost gloating attack.

Yet he led a life of infamy
And now he's alone as you can see
Quite abandoned and left to his fate
By his many friends of high estate

Ward is powerfully affected by this; he shades his eyes to try to hide how devastated he feels. The lights fade on everyone in the court except Ward, who sits alone, shattered. Slowly, he rises to his feet.

Chorus (*offstage, in the distance*)
You've never had it so good
You've never had it so often
Go and do what you never could
A brand new brother and sisterhood
You've never had it so good

Ward The judge was only halfway through his summing up, but I could see that it was all up with me; I realised that this case was not brought because of some undue interest in my sex life: it was a political revenge trial – and I'd had quite enough.

He begins to sing as he moves into the next scene.

SCENE ELEVEN

And now Stephen Ward is back in his house in Wimpole Mews; his manner is calm, serene almost.

Ward
There's no other way to heaven
Seems you have to die
I thought heaven could be found
This side of the sky

As he sings, he gathers together what he needs: a bottle of whisky, a glass of water and a couple of handfuls of barbiturates. He also lays out some writing paper and envelopes.

When you stand too close to the flame
It's your own fault no one else is to blame
There's no sense in fooling yourself with lies
Self-gratifying self-justifying lies

When you fly too close to the sun
Just be aware of the risks that you run
So-called friends are waiting to shoot you down
Watch your wings crumbling as you come tumbling
    down

I won't let them get me
I know what I have to do now
All because I came
Too close to the flame

He starts to take the first handful of Nembutal. In the distance, outside in the Mews, Christine Keeler appears and slowly and hesitantly begins to approach the house.

I shall miss the softness of skin
That moment when conversations begin
Capturing the beauty of someone new
Helping and healing that's a good feeling too

Yes I stood too close to the flame
But let me say I'm not dying of shame
I don't think I did anybody harm
Did what I could so maybe some good no harm

This is very easy
Hope I haven't disappointed
But you see I came
Too close to the flame

He continues taking the pills, washing them down with alternate swigs of water and whisky straight from the bottle. Meanwhile, Christine approaches, until she's right outside the front door. She raises a finger to press the doorbell: but at the last minute, her nerve fails her and she turns and walks sadly away.

    Ward finishes swallowing the pills, lights a cigarette, sits down and starts writing. After a time, he puts his letter in an envelope and seals it up. Then he rises, turns, and strolls back to take his place in the Chamber of Horrors line-up.

SCENE TWELVE

Back in the Chamber of Horrors in Blackpool, Ward hesitates and turns back to the audience.

Ward
Found me guilty as I knew they would
British justice – envied everywhere
Too late though to save the Government
Which it seems to me is only fair

Now I'm in the House of Wax instead of Paradise
A forty-carat bona-fide human sacrifice

He steps back into the line of waxworks, gives a wry smile and freezes.